Swansea's BURNING

Remembering the Three Nights' Blitz

by David Roberts

First published in Great Britain in 2011
Reprinted in 2016
by Bryngold Books Ltd.
100 Brynau Wood, Cimla,
Neath, South Wales SA11 3YQ.

www.bryngoldbooks.com

Typesetting, layout,
editing and design
by Bryngold Books

ISBN: 978-1-905900-42-8

Printed in Wales by
Gomer Press,
Llandysul, Ceredigion.

Contents

Salute to Swansea spirit   5

Sirens of disaster   7

Before the bombs   9

Countdown to catastrophe   17

The first night   25

The second night   33

The third night   43

The sky turned blood red   51

61   When dawn broke

69   Never the same again

77   Cold hard facts

87   Searching for safety

95   Why target Swansea?

103   Symbol of survival

111   Visits of destruction

119   Rising from the ashes

Appreciation

Swansea's Burning is a commemoration of one of the most significant events in the city's history — the Three Nights' Blitz of 1941.

Originally produced as the first ever hardback book on the subject to mark the 70th anniversary of the city's darkest days with a civic foreword by the Lord Mayor at the time, Councillor Richard Lewis, this special reprint was commissioned to mark the 75th anniversary. The aim of this was to continue to record the horror and heroism of the time for future generations. Swansea's Burning would not have been possible without the involvement and co-operation of a number of people and organisations. Among them are West Glamorgan Archive Service, source of many of the photographs; the guidance of Archivist Kim Collis and assistance of his staff was invaluable; Spencer Feeney, former editor-in-chief of the South Wales Evening Post, for allowing the use of images captured by the newspaper's photographers in those dark and distant days; JR Alban's book, The Three Nights' Blitz which was a useful reference tool; Gerald Gabb and David Beynon who kept matters on the straight and narrow with their proof reading; Stephen H Jones for his aviation expertise; Roy Kneath whose modern day pictorial portrayal shows the Swansea skyline at the time of original publication; Sid Kidwell, Ray Lewis, John Brayley, Des Barry, for their own individual, but invaluable contributions and finally, the staff of Bryngold Books for helping nurture the seed of an idea to fruition.

Salute to Swansea spirit

Many generations have walked Swansea's streets since the darkest chapter was etched into its long and proud history – the Three Nights' Blitz of February 1941.

During the midst of the Second World War this, perhaps more than at any other time, was when its people were stretched to their very limits and yet defiantly continued to battle on.

They have always been and will always remain determined and spirited, but never has this been so important for the community's survival as during the unrelenting aerial bombardment that changed the city's face forever on those fateful nights.

Swansea's Burning ensures that what those who were there endured in their brave quest for survival will never be forgotten. It combines a compelling narrative with many

The tower of St Mary's Church points skyward in defiance after the bombing symbolising Swansea's spirit.

fascinating images and facts from a variety of sources. It captures the essence of the Swansea that once was, so beloved of those who populated its narrow streets; focusses on each of the three nights; outlines the long quest to rise from the ashes and shows too, the look it has adopted for its march into the 21st Century.

With the passing of each year fewer and fewer of those who survived the

time when Swansea became an inferno, visible for miles around, remain to tell the tale. This book will revive fading memories, but just as importantly, will continue to tell the story for those not as familiar with the way things were before German bombs rained down during those harrowing wartime raids.

This book serves as an important commemoration. It is a lasting and fitting tribute to those who were there. It salutes those who worked so valiantly to tackle the fires started by the bombs, tend to the dying or treat the injured.

Swansea's Burning is a graphic and enduring reminder of the spirit of survival that runs through Swansea's veins. It will serve as a rich and invaluable history lesson for those who call this proud place their home.

David Roberts

Sirens of disaster

THE icy chill of a wartime winter's night offered few clues as to what lay ahead for Swansea, not a hint that it was about to be turned into a raging inferno — a town hotter than hell.

None of its residents could have anticipated the horror about to be unleashed onto their streets. None could have guessed that they would emerge from it to a scene of devastation — the face and character of the bustling town centre they knew and loved, obliterated.

Those same people were used to the sound of air raid sirens, but they could never have imagined that at 7.32pm on Wednesday, February 19, 1941, the

Swansea before the Three Nights' Blitz. Much of what is visible was either destroyed or badly damaged.

eerie wailing that drifted over the rooftops was heralding the beginning of the most catastrophic event in their town's history — the Three Nights' Blitz.

It was to become Swansea's darkest hour, three nights of terror when the German air force — the Luftwaffe — unleashed wave after wave of its deadly bombers on the town.

Each aircraft dumped a deadly cargo of bombs that blasted away centuries of Swansea's history and changed the lives of its inhabitants forever.

A relentless rain of explosives fell in three consecutive nights of bombs and blazes; nights when bravery, grit and determination stood tall amid scenes of death, injury and awesome destruction. The bombs alone were not responsible for the

eventual destruction and devastation. Much of this resulted from the ferocity of the firestorm that swept through the narrow streets. The conflagration was so great it could be seen from many miles around.

Destruction was so widespread and total that it was some time before people could even take it all in. It's a wonder that the town survived such a pounding, but the determination of its people saw it through.

It was to be many years before Swansea would even begin to rise from the ashes, but while it waited it could still hold its head up high.

The intention of this book is to record the horror and heroism of those dark and distant days and salute all those who survived such an unforgettable chapter in Swansea's history; those who battled for its very existence and those who paid the supreme sacrifice in doing so.

A true spirit of survival
displayed by its stunned
people, saw Swansea
through its darkest hour.

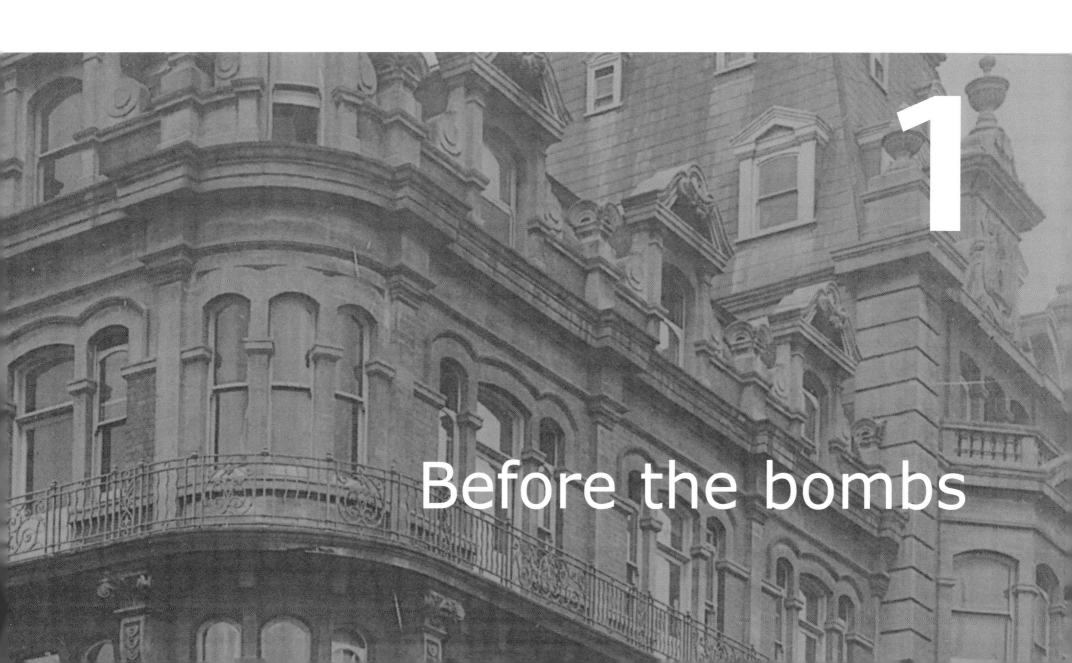

1

Before the bombs

Looking from the forecourt of High Street station across into Alexandra Road, 1925.

THE bustling Swansea that existed before the outbreak of the Second World War was very different to that of the 21st Century. It was a typical Welsh trading town that depended heavily on its location by the sea.

The town centre streets of the long-established seaport were mainly narrow and lined with a clutter of small stores each plying its own trade. There was a selection of grander establishments too. Along with the market they satisfied most needs.

These busy thoroughfares were lined by buildings that were undeniably interesting in architectural terms, often far more appealing than their replacements. This was a reflection of the town's prosperous past, a history born out of its role in the very vanguard of the industrial revolution. The different styles of many of its buildings also showed just how much interaction there had been between Swansea and trading partners in foreign lands. The influence is still visible in some of the architecture that survives. A history lesson in itself.

One of the most imposing of these grand buildings was that occupied by the prestigious Ben Evans department store. This was not simply the Harrods of Swansea, but the whole of Wales.

Some buildings remain from those grand pre-war days, but they can only hint at what was lost during the wartime bombing that changed totally the special character that had evolved with Swansea's growing up.

There is no secret as to why Swansea was so grand in its time. It was all about money and prosperity. Long before the outbreak of war however, Swansea had seen its peak in the kind of financial fortunes on which its proud pedigree was created. But it still looked and felt the part.

Although the town had its share of less well-off residents, there was plenty of money in other families. It had been generated from the earliest 18th Century times of the Industrial Revolution and through the 19th Century too. It was the money of productivity, of coal and copper, oil and export.

Businesses thrived and prospered in Temple Street, Goat Street, Orange Street, Waterloo Street and many other long-gone areas.

Around them were countless streets of residential properties often housing families far bigger than those of later years, something which also contributed to the bustle of the place. There were no out-of-town shopping centres then, this was the shared hub of commerce and community.

Now, many years after the destruction of such streets by relentless German bombing, few people can recall all the buildings of the old town centre with great clarity.

Memories of what poet Dylan Thomas referred to as his 'ugly, lovely, town', are strong enough, however, to provide evidence that this was a town proud of its heritage.

This was a pride that not only assisted its wartime survival, but helped it grow into a vibrant city.

There was no secret as to why
Swansea was so grand in its time.
It was all about productivity,
prosperity and money.

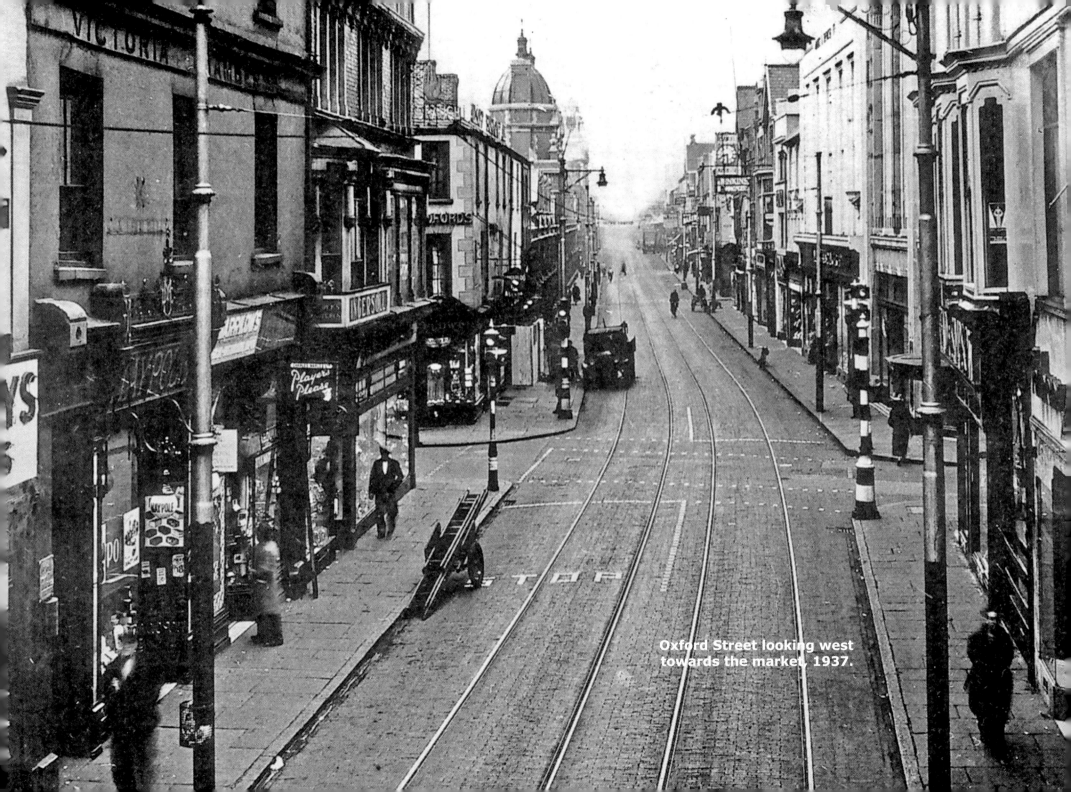
Oxford Street looking west towards the market. 1937.

The majestic exterior of Ben Evans' Castle Street department store, regarded by many people at the time as the Harrods of Wales.

Oxford Street, showing the market with its grand main entrance during 1938 before its wartime bombing.

There was not a single hint
that with each minute that passed,
the horrors of warfare were
winging their way ever closer.

2

Countdown to catastrophe

A policeman patrols his beat along College Street, mid-1930s.

Stead & Simpson's shoe shop on the corner of Waterloo Street and Oxford Street in the mid-1930s.

Temple Street, looking down into Oxford Street, late 1930s.

A shiver ran down the spine of snow-dusted Swansea as it tucked itself in for another long, dark winter's night. The icy chill drilled into the bone of the stragglers hurrying home along the tightly woven, town centre streets fringed with a patchwork of buildings each as different as the people living behind their closed doors.

Like everyone else, everywhere else, in Britain on that distant night they were at war. Few clues would have been necessary to determine the subject of conversation in the flickering firelight at many a hearth. But there was no hint as those same innocent men, women and children chatted, that with each minute that passed, the horrors of warfare were winging their way ever closer to their own front doors. By morning their world would be a far different place. Each comforting tick-tock of their mantel clocks was marking the countdown to Swansea's darkest hour: the most significant catastrophe in its history and yet an event that showed its people at their finest. The three nights of relentless bombing that was to follow would portray the community as one whose inhabitants could call on seemingly endless reserves of true grit, guts and determined spirit of survival like no other.

When it came to the shock and awe of warfare, on that unforgettable night — Wednesday, February 19, 1941, it was their turn. That night and the two terrifying repeats that followed would see men, women and children alike, erase from their minds concerns about the cold. Their thoughts instead would be filled with raw, undefined and unimaginable horror as their town was consumed by flames.

They had no warning of what lay ahead. No expectation that they had already taken their last look at the Swansea they knew and loved; no anticipation even, of the cargo of anguish and heartache that was rumbling through the night sky heading straight for their seaport. They would experience emptiness akin to the loss of a loved one and in a way that was exactly what they were about to suffer.

For as the few brave enough to venture onto the streets hurried about their missions in the darkness, the men who wore the wings of the German Luftwaffe were just as intent about theirs; determined to leave their own unforgettable calling card with their unsuspecting victims.

Swansea may well have been colder than a mortuary slab that night, but before the clock on the sentinel-like St Mary's Church tower had chimed midnight the townspeople would have given scant thought to the cold.

Instead their chill would be induced by fear as the town burned, turning into an inferno as explosion after explosion rocked its very core and razed familiar buildings. None of the town's residents could have guessed that they would emerge from the living nightmare about to be unleashed on their streets to discover their town centre transformed into a pile of smouldering

St Mary's Church, before the war. The vehicles on the left are parked in St Mary's Street, those on the right in Fisher Street.

ruins and rubble reminiscent of the remains of a gigantic bonfire.

When the Luftwaffe crews had dropped their final bombs and turned their aircraft for home they left behind a burning beacon where once had been a maze of shopping streets. Its glow was their reminder of the firestorm they had created thousands of feet below them.

It was also an indelible full stop in Swansea's proud history.

There was plenty of bustle in College Street in 1929.

PREPARE NOW. DON'T TAKE A CHANCE

HAVE READY — buckets of water, a shovel on a broom-handle, or something similar, and a hatchet. A ladder (or "steps") is also useful. Keep your torch in good condition and make sure you know where there is a stirrup-pump. Make sure your attic is clear of everything that may catch fire. Remove all rubbish, paper, loose pieces of wood and other inflammable material.

When resources were stretched to the limit, it was often left to householders to do their own firefighting. This guide above is typical of many that appeared in wartime newspapers. It shows the array of handy implements that the Government suggested residents should have readily at hand to help fend off the dangers of stray incendiary bombs and the destructive fires they could cause.

Gower Street, much of which was destroyed by the Three Nights' Blitz of wartime, February 1941, presents a more peaceful scene in the mid-1930s.

The explosive cocktail of bombs that rained down from the sky blasted centuries of Swansea's history to smithereens.

3

The first night

Streets everywhere were filled with fallen masonry.

All that remained of the Adelaide Hotel in Adelaide Place.

A burned out vehicle among the rubble of properties in Goat Street.

After the initial warning on February 19, it was 16 long minutes before the first bombs began falling and nearly three and a half hours before the final Heinkel III aircraft that had carried them, banked away and headed home to its French base.

The townspeople were used to the sound of air raid sirens — there had been enough previous raids to remove any doubt they may have had in their minds — but this time at 7.23pm on Wednesday, February 19, 1941, their eerie wail heralded the start of the most destructive event in their town's history. At 7.37pm a further warning was given that a raid was imminent. Two minutes later the Heinkel III bombers began their pounding.

Each heavily laden aircraft that crossed the Swansea sky dumped a deadly cargo of bombs, an explosive cocktail that blasted centuries of Swansea history to smithereens.

The residents could not fail to hear the aircraft as their engines thundered overhead. It sounded as though there were hundreds of them. The drone of their engines was so loud it could even be heard above the almost non-stop thud of explosions and telling sounds produced by breaking glass and falling masonry as buildings tumbled.

It was later learned that on that fateful night 73 German aircraft had taken off from bases in Brittany, Normandy and to the north of Paris. Unexpected events encountered during their nocturnal aerial expedition resulted in several breaking off to attack alternative targets, and three others to abort the mission, so that a total of 61 deadly aircraft actually took part in the eventual attack on Swansea.

The first aircraft to reach the target zone, began its bombing run at 7.39pm from an altitude of between 2,600 and 3,600 metres.

This strike started fires which were themselves bombed at 8.02 pm by the follow-up force. These aircraft

succeeded in lighting up the target town even further by depositing no fewer than 9,216 incendiary bombs on what was no longer a sleepy Welsh seaport.

Successive waves of bombers continued the onslaught depositing a lethal mixture of 49.2 tons of high explosive bombs and 15.72 tons of incendiaries until they had no more to drop. The last marauding aircraft turned for home at 11.03pm. Eventually the all-clear and the relief it brought with it, was sounded at one minute before midnight.

All-clear the message may have been, but the departing raiders had left the huddled streets in total chaos and confusion. As the flames of the many resultant fires reached higher and higher into the night sky the damage below them grew and many asked themselves how Swansea could endure or survive such a lethal beating. Such questions would carry even more significance after the two further consecutive nights of aerial bombardment that followed.

Hodges Corner at the junction of High Street and College Street.

Smoke pours from smouldering buildings at the junction of Castle Street and College Street in the aftermath of a raid.

HOW TO DEAL WITH A FIRE BOMB IN THE OPEN

1. The easiest way to carry a sandbag is to sling it over your shoulder.

2. When approaching the fire bomb shield your face with the sandbag.

3. Don't empty the sandbag on the fire bomb. Place the sandbag on the bomb.

4. When you have covered the fire bomb GET AWAY as quickly as you can.

Wartime newspapers encouraged their readers to be prepared for any eventuality during bombing raids. The articles here were intended to give people a fighting chance in coping with incendiary bombs both inside and outside their homes.

HOW TO DEAL WITH A FIRE BOMB INDOORS

1. Always enter a burning room on hands and knees. Open the door slowly to avoid possible bursts of flame and fumes. Keep your head back as you open the door.

2. Those who man the stirrup-pump should stay OUTSIDE the burning room. One pumps, another brings water.

3. In attacking the fire bomb crawl towards it, head well down, face shielded. Take whatever cover you can, such as a table or chair.

4. If furniture or hangings are on fire, deal with them first, damping them down with the *jet*. Then turn the *spray* on to the fire bomb.

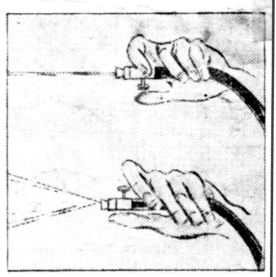

5. How to operate the pump nozzle showing how to change over quickly from jet to spray.

Tiredness and fatigue were not
in the vocabulary of those
struggling to retrieve normality
from the smouldering ruins.

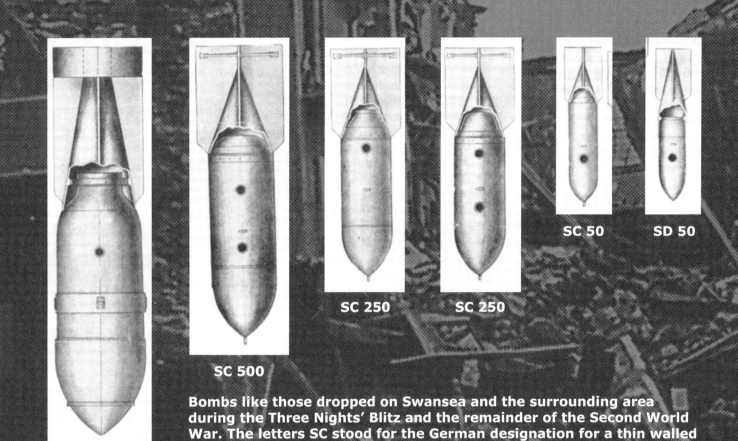

SC 1000

SC 500

SC 250

SC 250

SC 50

SD 50

Bombs like those dropped on Swansea and the surrounding area during the Three Nights' Blitz and the remainder of the Second World War. The letters SC stood for the German designation for a thin walled high explosive bomb followed by the bomb's weight in kilograms and SD for a thick walled high explosive fragmentation bomb.

These buildings in Castle Street remained but displayed obvious signs of an inferno that had ripped out their heart.

A lone figure alongside a wrecked car in Goat Street at its junction with Oxford Street, left and Temple Street, right.

Ruined St Mary's Church, surrounded by utter devastation.

By daybreak on Thursday, February 20 life in Swansea had changed forever.
Those who ventured near the town centre were greeted with acrid smoke from the fires that still burned; streets blocked with fallen masonry and strange gaps where familiar buildings had stood.

It was all difficult to take in. Even harder to comprehend would have been the fact that the preceeding night of hell was to be repeated twice more before they would be allowed anything like a respite.

Work continued throughout the day to tackle the results of the German onslaught. Tiredness and fatigue were not words to be found in the vocabulary of those struggling to retrieve normality from the ruins. As the winter darkness closed in few would have believed it had they been told that more Luftwaffe bombers were already on the tarmac of their airfields loaded with a further deadly cargo. Once again on this second night, the wailing of air raid sirens filled the air. They had started their warning at 7.40pm. After eight minutes the red warning, for raid imminent, was given. Two minutes later the bombers swept in. This time, the first wave of incoming Heinkels began their approach at 7.50pm and again unleashed a mixed cargo of incendiary and high explosive bombs. Further waves of these destructive flying machines punctuated the night sky, each relieving itself of its weighty carnage-causing cargo before stopping at around ll.45pm.

On this second night an even larger aerial force was tasked to target Swansea. This time 88 Heinkel aircraft took off from their bases; 16 eventually aborted their missions and eight others dropped their bombs on alternative targets. However, 64 got through to Swansea where, between 7.50pm and 12.24am they dropped a total of 58.4 tons of high explosive bombs and 19,994 incendiaries which again played a fateful part in illuminating the target for subsequent aircraft and also started fire after fire.

German reports recorded that while the anti-aircraft defences on the previous night had been virtually non-existent, on this occasion the flak which sliced its way up from the darkness below was slightly heavier, although still largely ineffective. By now the defence, rescue and fire-fighting squads were stretched to the limit, though they never gave up.

Shortly after the attack began the ARP controller was forced to call for aid from rescue services in Neath, Port Talbot, Llanelli and Merthyr. Eventually fire tenders were queuing up at a location in Llansamlet waiting to be directed to those parts of the town where they were most needed.

The all-clear was finally sounded at 12.24am. Shocked and stunned, by their ordeal the people of Swansea could have been forgiven once again for daring to imagine that they had been dealt the worst.

But little did they realise that on this night, as they still struggled to come to terms with the devastation of the previous evening's raid, the town was still being softened up.

A concerned mum's hand reaches down to check the operation of a baby's respirator on her young daughter. Another youngster wears a different type of gas mask while playing on her tricycle, both during wartime 1940s Swansea.

The morning after the Three Nights' Blitz and the rescue and demolition teams set about clearing the streets of rubble. Woolworth's High Street store is on the left.

Heinkel 111

Aircraft like these here
were used in the bombing
raids on Swansea.

Junkers 88

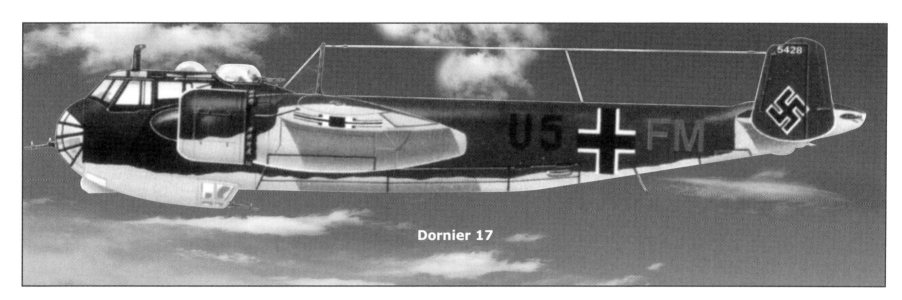

Dornier 17

Luftwaffe aircraft used in raids on Swansea

Category	Heinkel 111	Junkers 88	Dornier 17
Crew	5	2-6	4
Engines	2 x 2,000hp	2 x Jumo 211J-1 or J-2 1,000-kW 1,340hp	2 x 1,700hp
Wingspan	71ft (22m)	65ft 7.5in (20m)	62ft 4in (19m)
Length	58ft 3in (18m)	51ft (16m)	56ft 9.25in (17m)
Height	21ft 6in (7m)	15ft 9in (5m)	16ft 5in (5m)
Bomb Load	4,400lb (2,000kg)	2,205lb (1,002kg)	3,300lb (1,500kg)
Loaded Weight	38,200lb (17,363kg)	26,686lb (12,130kg)	33,070lb (15,000kg)
Max. Speed	258mph (415km/hr)	280mph (451km/hr)	265mph (426km/hr)
Max. Range	745 miles (1,200km)	1,453 miles (2,339km)	721 miles (1,160km)
Max. Ceiling	25,590ft (7,800m)	26,500ft (8,080m)	26,740ft (8,150m)
Production	7,300	15,000	1,730

**Fires still smouldered in the ruins,
long after the bombers had gone.**

One of the few surviving photographs that captured the uncontrollable firestorm created by German bombs dropped during the Three Nights' Blitz.

Blazes merged into a devastating
firestorm that roared through
the narrow streets, devouring building
after building as it went.

5

The third night

Two brave firefighters play their hoses on burning buildings as the firestorm intensifies.

Mount Pleasant Chapel stands defiant among the ruins of Heathfield Street and Gower Street.

Ruined Wesley Chapel, College Street.

44

As the bombs whistled down across historic Swansea town on the third night's raid the crews of the Luftwaffe warbirds dropping them may well have wondered about the families, just like their own, on whom they were inflicting such a torrent of terror.

But this was war and they had orders to follow. Later in the war perhaps they suffered when the Allies began similar bombing raids on their homes.

Meanwhile, thousands of feet below them on the icy ground, most of those fighting the fires, often with the most basic of equipment, had already been toiling for two nights with little time to stop and draw breath.

Those brave and heroic men and women knew that the waves of bombers droning menacingly above them in the darkened Swansea skies were there for the kill. The pummelling of the preceding two nights could be likened to a prize-fighter softening up his hapless opponent for the final knock-out blow. That, without doubt, was the intention of the flyers on their third visit.

For all that, the resolve of those on the ground to do their best, held firm. At least it did until the eruption of an uncontrollable firestorm that, at an alarming pace, assumed such tremendous dimensions that efforts to combat the flames reaching higher and higher from the burning pile, proved futile. The fire crews braced themselves in hope. They had done their best. They could do no more.

On the third night, with the town centre already dominated by charred ruins and the still-smoking, rubbled remains of what were once popular shopping venues, 59 more heavily laden aircraft attacked Swansea, dropping 47.6 tons of high explosives and a further 20,436 incendiaries.

The 'raiders imminent' warning sounded at 7.30pm and the first wave of bombers was overhead barely 10 minutes later. The raid, during which extensive structural damage was caused through widespread fires, lasted what seemed like an eternity, before ending at 12.40 am.

On the first two nights a superhuman effort by everyone concerned had, incredibly, managed to keep the resulting fires under control. But by the third, the prolonged stress on the defenders, coupled with the damage countless high explosive bombs had done to water and gas mains, made fire-fighting virtually impossible.

The resultant blazes, many fuelled by fractured gas mains, merged into a devastating firestorm that overwhelmed those fearlessly fighting them and roared through the time-worn, narrow streets, reaching from one side to the other, devouring building after building as they went. Some observers claimed every building from Castle Street right down to Oxford Street was ablaze.

As the flames licked skywards, the glow was visible for many miles around. Those who saw it from afar needed no telling that the crimson sky spectacle they were witnessing was a

A mobile canteen provides welcome refreshment for some of those who battled so bravely, to save Swansea.

town writhing in the agony of death and destruction. Even with the brave and gallant help once again of firefighters drawn from outside the town, it was not until well into the daylight hours of February 22 that the roaring blazes which had engulfed everything in their path were finally tamed. Charred ruins, twisted metal girders and mountains of rubble were all that remained.

Two Luftwaffe aircraft failed to return to their base after this mission, but it was a small price to pay for the magnitude of their mission's success.

It was to be Swansea's lowest point. Not just in the war, but in its entire history. A staggering 41 acres of the town centre had been wiped out and much more rendered all but useless. It was to be years before the town would begin to rise from the ashes.

However, if the aerial bombardment had been aimed at pummelling Swansea into submission, then it had failed. There was never any thought of giving in. The spirit of its people survived.

Damping down the fires at the Ben Evans store the morning after it was blitzed.

4

The second night

Plenty of bombs, but not a blitz

Although the Germans dropped some 800 high explosive bombs and 30,000 incendiaries, killing 230 people and injuring 409, while making 7,000 homeless and destroying 41 acres of the town's commercial centre, the three-night attack was not officially classified as a blitz.

As strange as it might have seemed to those who endured them, the larger raids on Swansea were not even considered to be major attacks. Both the British and German authorities defined a major attack as one in which 100 tons of high explosive bombs were dropped.

On the three nights of February 19, 20, and 21, 1941 the quantities dropped were 49.2, 58.4 and 47.6 tons respectively. Some of the bombs dropped are shown here. Often incendiary bombs would be dropped in a canister containing dozens of bomblets, like those on the right.

The rough scale of these can be seen alongside with an enlargement of one of the fire bombs.

The weight of the high-explosive bombs dropped on Swansea varied from 50 kilograms up to 1,000 kilogrammes.

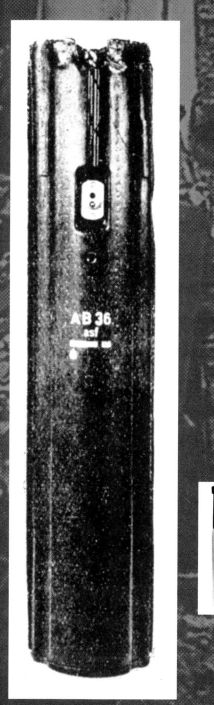

The bombers left behind a burning beacon where once had been a maze of shopping streets. Its glow was a full stop in Swansea's proud history.

6

The sky turned blood red

Firefighters pour water on the flames that continued to ravage the Ben Evans store even at daybreak.

A narrow route was cleared to allow vehicles through Castle Bailey Street.

Temple Street, blocked by fallen masonry.

The ominous crimson glow that frighteningly illuminated the February night sky told Swansea's neighbours all they needed to know. People in Neath, Port Talbot, Llanelli, and Carmarthen, even Pembrokeshire and across the Bristol Channel in Devon, saw the distant darkness turn a menacing, blood red as it reflected the flames of the fires the bombs had caused.

As they watched in horror they could only fear the worst. But even that would not have stretched their imagination far enough. The town centre was hotter than a furnace. The smell of burning material filled the air. Streets almost vanished under billowing clouds of dry, choking, acrid smoke and particles of soft, sooty ash settled on every remaining surface.

Amid all this, high-explosive and incendiary bombs continued to fall, hindering the efforts of those heroically struggling to rescue the trapped, or help the injured and homeless. They battled through each night and the day that followed under the threat of more bombs, fire and dangerously tottering, ruined buildings, to fulfill their vital roles.

For these bravehearts on the ground throughout this aerial siege, sleep was not an option. They needed to keep going; they had to keep going; and somehow they did.

On the third night firefighters from outside Swansea had been drafted in to help battle the blazes. But the valiant efforts of these extra crews to quell the flames were hampered by a desperate shortage of water.

The cause of this was the destruction of water supply mains across the town by high explosive bombs on the Wednesday and Thursday nights. Where water could be located in a frantic bid to quench the town's seemingly endless thirst, getting it to the scene of fires presented another problem. Many miles of water hoses criss-crossed the streets and stretched from both the North and South docks in an effort to keep up some supply of water. These snaking supply lines were continually being torn apart and severed by the rain of high-explosive bombs. Consequently, firefighters were often compelled to stand and watch helplessly as buildings burned themselves out.

To add to the difficulties of operating the Civil Defence services, countless roads became blocked either by gigantic bomb craters, rubble from ravaged buildings or unexploded bombs. Often rescue, first aid or Auxiliary Fire Service vehicles had to cover long, circuitous, and more importantly time-consuming, routes in order to reach their destination. Matters took a further turn for the worse when the main rescue and defence depot was ravaged by direct hits with eight high-explosive bombs, causing further chaos and extensive damage to buildings, vital transport and equipment. This was a fight for survival like no other seen in Wales at any time throughout the war.

The scale of the damage to Swansea town centre can be judged by this view looking east along Oxford Street with the David Evans store in the centre and former Evening Post building in the distance.

Looking up Wind Street at all that was left standing of the Ben Evans store. Smoke from the many fires still smouldering in the rubble that was once the town filled the air.

Some of the firefighters whose heroic exploits helped Swansea survive the blazes that followed wartime bombing.

An anti-aircraft unit sends its shells skyward towards German aerial raiders.

Swansea was defended by 24 anti-aircraft batteries like this one during the Three Nights' Blitz, but it seemed they proved ineffective. German reports suggested that their Luftwaffe bombers had encountered little resistance from their guns.

Words of

'**We COWERED** under the stairs as the **bombs** rained down'

'The *inferno* was so great fire fighters couldn't get near some BURNING buildings'

'Everyone was SCARED stiff. It was something no one had **experienced**'

What some of those who survived said.

witness

'They were TERRIBLE nights when boys became men'

'It was *terrifying*. Streets were full of flames, smoke and a HORRID burning smell'

'People were RUNNING around screaming as buildings collapsed'

What some of those who survived said.

Men and women
were stealing shoes
out of a smashed shop window.
It was a disgusting sight.

7

When dawn broke

Waterloo Street — lost forever.

Fisher Street looking towards the Ben Evans Store.

Once this had been the thriving store of The South Wales Furnishers company.

62

WHEN the pale, smoke-grey dawn broke after the third night of bombing, the town centre lay devastated — a mass of rubble, twisted metal and still smouldering buildings.

Roads, heaped with masonry and riddled with craters, were impassable. There was widespread damage to sewers and electric cables. Telephones were out of order and 15 schools were either destroyed or badly damaged.

Far worse, were the reports that 230 people had been killed in the three nights of carnage, with many more injured. As many as 7,000 people were made homeless.

The catalogue of destruction was endless. Shops, including 171 selling foodstuffs, were destroyed and the market, whose butchers alone supplied more than 22,000 customers, was reduced to a charred shell. Gas and water were cut off, making cooking difficult. Communal feeding centres were set up and water-tank lorries drove through the area with badly needed supplies. Emergency service personnel, who had worked like Trojans, with only a few hours of rest during the previous 72 hours were soon at work again attending to the grim task of sifting through mangled, smouldering structures and debris for survivors.

As buildings not toppled by the bombs were made safe, barricades were erected to seal off the town centre because of the danger of unexploded bombs. Although damage to buildings was extensive, casualties were not as heavy as had initially been feared. Loss of life was comparatively low given the extent of the structural devastation because of the limited danger zone of the average bomb explosion, the spread of the population and the wide area over which the bombs were scattered.

That was no consolation to those who survived, had lost loved ones or all of their treasured possessions, but in a way it was a fact to be grateful for.

In the days following the raid, tales of bravery and heroism were told and re-told. Amid the carnage and destruction there had been an almost superhuman struggle for survival. At one point it was said that there was only one water pump in the centre of town which was working.

Teams of firefighters did what they could against unthinkable odds. One group incredibly managed to stem the tide of angry flames flowing down Oxford Street.

A number of these had close calls with death. One was wiped out by a blast. On another occasion a shell landed within a few feet of one fireman. Miraculously, another crew only escaped being blown up by a delayed action bomb because they were called to another incident.

Everyone had their tales. An ARP warden told how he was straight outside after the siren went, checking there were no lights showing and telling people to get into shelters.

"Incendiary bombs were falling everywhere you looked. It was a terrible experience," he said.

"They dropped a lot on Kilvey Hill. So much so that it looked like

It was beyond belief for people that their beloved town had been transformed into a collection of tottering ruins.

Blackpool illuminations. A bomb fell just 20 yards from me in a lane separating Pentregethin Road and Fern Street. The blast went straight up the lane and no damage was done."

One woman witnessed a land mine dropping in Oxford Street.

"The force of the blast knocked big shop windows out like ninepins," she said.

"A group of people started looting a shoe shop near the old Macowards store. Men and women were stealing shoes out of the window.

"We looked on in amazement. Others joined them then. It was a disgusting sight."

It was one of the few occasions where this kind of incident was reported to have occurred.

Deserted and devastated the town centre as it looked in the aftermath of the bombing.

The ruined centre of Swansea after Luftwaffe bombers
had accomplished their gruesome task and headed home.

The effects of the bombing on St Mary's Church. It was later rebuilt and reconsecrated in 1959.

The roofless ruins of St Mary's Church. Most of the buildings around it had been destroyed.

Other Welsh towns suffered
badly throughout the war,
but it was Swansea that took
the hardest hit.

8

Never the same again

More than 25,000 meals were provided for the homeless in the days after the Three Nights' Blitz.

Twisted and buckled steel girders of buildings in Portland Street are evidence of the intensity of the fires.

Looking westwards along Oxford Street.

As the flames subsided and the smoke slowly cleared to reveal the true scale of the destruction, the words on everyone's lips were that things would never be the same again in Swansea. There was hardly an aspect of life in the town that wasn't, in some way, affected by the Three Nights' Blitz it had endured.

True, there had been other aerial incursions, and enough to convince people in the town that when the air raid warnings sounded it was not something to be taken lightly.

But the Three Nights' Blitz that came at the end of February 1941 was different. Much different. This time the German bombers had not just contented themselves with simple hit and run tactics. Instead they hung around. Wave after wave of aircraft made sure that their explosive cargo hit home — and hard. As a result shops, offices, places of worship, hotels, cinemas as well as homes were all seriously damaged or completely destroyed.

In addition to this, around 15 schools, including Dynevor School, Swansea Grammar School and the huge Ben Evans department store were among landmarks at best seriously damaged, at worst destroyed.

The infrastructure of the town was in total disarray. Everything seemed to hang on a thread: a thread of morale that survived to hold things together.

Families gathered around battery-powered radio sets to gain every scrap of information they could. They were left only with imagination to paint a picture of what was happening elsewhere. They knew enough however, information learned the hard way, that life really was never going to be the same again in Swansea. Though they realised they had survived an unbelievable onslaught, the true extent of the devastation was something that took a great deal longer to sink in. Some clearance work got underway almost immediately. Generally though it would be weeks before blocked streets were finally cleared sufficiently to allow safe passage along them for both vehicles and pedestrians.

Some businesses relocated fairly quickly to premises on the fringe of the former shopping and commercial area of the town. Many were now fighting their own battle for survival. Others simply ceased trading.

Other Welsh towns were targeted throughout the war, but Swansea took the hardest hit; the hammer blow.

As darkness fell on the night of February 22 every citizen of the battered town was probably thinking the same: that they were in for another night of terror, another visit from the bombers. Miraculously it didn't happen and with the dawn came a noticeable sigh of relief.

From that point a strange sense of normality began to return. Everyone was aware however that nothing would ever be the same again. And, decades later, despite much rebuilding, it isn't. There was little repair, but much replacement.

A group of Royal Engineers prepare to blow up all that remained of a once proud Swansea store.

Damaged shops in Union Street after the heavy bombing.

Controlled explosions like this one, executed by Army engineers,
were used to bring down the remains of ruined buildings.

Still standing, but just a burned out shell, the Lloyds Bank building in Temple Street, viewed through the rubbled remains of the Ben Evans department store.

**The most important target
of the aerial raiders
remained intact — morale.
Swansea was determined to defy defeat.**

9

Cold hard facts

This house in Ffynone received a direct hit.

Dynevor School, one of many seriously damaged.

Everywhere you looked there was rubble.

Over the three nights of attacks, 230 people died. This was more than half the total killed in bombing raids on Swansea throughout the six long and difficult years of the Second World War.

In the worst single incident, 46 people were killed and 44 were injured when a stick of six bombs fell on houses in Teilo Crescent, Mayhill.

Apart from the fatalities of the Three Nights' Blitz a further 409 people were injured, 232 of them seriously, and some 7,000 people lost their homes in the raids, which lasted a total of 13 hours and 48 minutes.

During that time around 800 high explosive bombs fell on the town along with more than 49,000 incendiary bombs. A staggering 857 buildings were totally destroyed and a further 11,000 damaged.

The districts of Townhill, Manselton, Brynhyfryd and St Thomas, Bonymaen, Morriston, Llansamlet, Landore, Hafod, Danygraig and Mount Pleasant were among places also hit, but not on the scale of the town centre. There, the main shopping area was devastated and the market was gutted. Major stores turned into piles of rubble. Everything inside them was consumed in the final firestorm.

Rescuers had battled bravely in the most dangerous conditions.
They often carried on in heroic desperation to save their beloved town while bombs continued to rain down. Almost everything they did was hampered by craters and debris.

In all 48 major sewers and drains were damaged, 47 gas mains, 57 water mains, 31 electricity cables and six telephone cables. With the water supply disrupted, 22 tanker lorries and bowsers were brought in to distribute fresh water. Mobile canteens and huge makeshift cafes provided vital meals.

Raw figures may spell out the cold statistics of this most tragic period in Swansea's history, but they fail to convey anything of the human pain and suffering that was inflicted during those terrible three nights. By the morning of February 22, the information from reports on the previous night's incidents revealed that the town's essential supplies were in a disastrous predicament. Swansea was as close to breaking point as it would ever be.

For those who struggled through the fear and ferocity of the Blitz, and survived, the memory of it never left them. For them it was one of those experiences that are never forgotten.

"There's nothing left," some said at the time. And they were almost right. But the most important target of the warring night raiders remained — Swansea's morale.

On the BBC Home Service's Six O'clock News, residents reported that far from being affected, it was higher than ever. They were right. Yes people were angry, but they were also undeniably determined to defy defeat. And it was through this fact more than any other that Swansea managed to pull through and survive the direst ordeal it was ever likely to encounter.

The burned out shell of the once bustling Swansea Market.

Teilo Crescent, Mayhill, showing the devastating effects of the Luftwaffe bombs that fell on the second night.

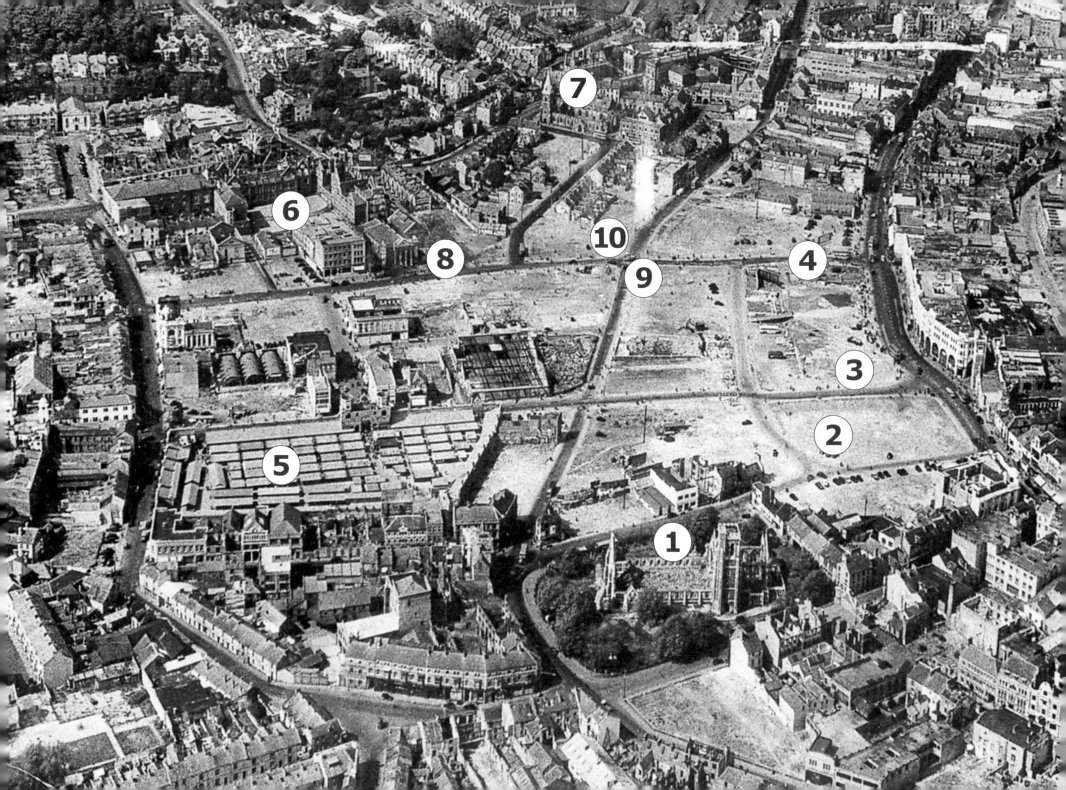

THE FLATTENED TOWN

1. St Mary's Church
2. Ben Evans department store
3. Lloyds Bank
4. Wesley Chapel
5. Temporary market
6. Dynevor School
7. Trinity Church
8. Mount Pleasant Church
9. Kingsway roundabout
10. Site of Dragon Hotel

83

This fire appliance, seen in 1965 on one of its last trips in service was known as the Big Six. Now restored, it helped fight the fires of the Three Nights' Blitz.

One of the vehicles pressed into service as an ambulance at Manselton ambulance depot, during the Three Nights' Blitz of February 1941, with some of those who helped crew it.

During the blitz, the town's
rat population didn't need
a pied piper to lead them away —
they scuttled off of their own accord.

10

Searching for safety

Two typical young evacuees.

Residents carry their belongings on the daily exodus.

For youngsters evacuation was a troublesome time.

People living on the Gower Peninsula were among those who could only stand and watch helplessly as the effects of the bombs caused fires that lit up the night sky around the centre of Swansea.

By the second night of the blitz the area in which they lived became a target too. Not for the bombers however, but endless columns of people trudging out of the town in what for a while became an almost daily exodus. A quest for safety.

Many of those living on the residential fringes of the town were beginning to fear for their lives and seemed to share the view that the further they went from the town centre the better their chances of survival during further bombing.

Thousands of them grabbed what they could in the way of blankets and quilts and headed for the comparative safety of the Gower countryside. Many shared tales of their experiences with folk they met on the way.

In late afternoon long strings of people began leaving the city on foot as there was no transport available.

After what was an arduous trudge, families, often with young children, would reach the open countryside at around six o'clock and huddle in groups in fields and under hedges.

They would wait, watch and wonder whether they would have a home to return to the following day after a raid, if one came. Some did, many didn't. But at least they were alive.

For many families this exodus simply meant a trip down the garden path to the perceived safety of their corrugated Anderson shelters. Often however the retreat to such hideaways was only sparked by an air raid siren and they left it until the last minute before seeking refuge in them.

Ironically just a short while before the Three Nights' Blitz, Swansea had seen the arrival of numbers of evacuees from the London area. They had come to Swansea to be safe and yet here they were now in the thick of the bombing again. Many of these youngsters were perplexed to find themselves in the middle of what was even greater danger than they had left behind. They could have been forgiven for wondering exactly what was going on as they were either moved on or joined the regular march for safety.

And while countless children were evacuated to Swansea during the war many local youngsters were themselves evacuated from the town in the months following the blitz. They boarded trains which took them into west and mid-Wales. When they eventually returned to their families, they returned to a town they hardly recognised from the one that they had left behind.

But it wasn't just people who were leaving the town. There was another exodus too. During the blitz, the town's rat population didn't need a pied piper to lead them away — they scuttled off of their own accord.

A woman who witnessed thousands of rats scuttling up Sketty Road towards Singleton Park told how she hid in a garden until they had passed.

An Anderson shelter which took a near direct hit from a high explosive bomb. The family inside were rescued unscathed.

One Swansea family gathers around an Anderson shelter in its garden.

Night Attack On Welsh Coast

SAVAGE BOMBING OF TOWN CENTRE

GERMAN raiders operating in small numbers kept anti-aircraft gunners busy in Wales during the night. There was a raid of some hours in one area. High explosive and incendiary bombs were dropped. Coastal places were attacked.

Later reports show the full extent of the savage and indiscriminate bombing of this town, which is on the coast. The bombs fell in the centre of the town. Fires were started in many buildings, and cast a red glare in the sky. One shopping street is badly damaged and many buildings are gutted. Streets in the centre of to. 21,129 debris.

According to the Air M attacks were directed mainly

SWANSEA MAIN TARGET OF NAZI RAIDERS

Wife of Alderman Dies After Rescue

SWANSEA was the
mur target of the Nazi
res were started
rcial buildings
building, and a
school and a
ur incendiaries
ce.
17 people had
d totalled 36,
P. personnel.
of Alderman
. Alderman
the North of
ith Mr. and
nd brother-

MURDER RAIDERS SWANSEA

own Valiantly Faces Another Night Ordeal

U.S.
V

200

Whit

BRAINS OF WALES
ESTABLISHED 1713

South Wales
Evening Post

No. 21,130

SATURDAY, FEBRUARY 22, 1941

[Registered at the G.P.O. as a Newspaper]

THREE-HALFPENCE

SWANSEA AGAIN: SEVERE DAMAGE IN TOWN'S THIRD NIGHT ORDEAL

Waves of Raiders Shower Fire Bombs and High Explosives

Churches, Business Premises and Houses Suffer

SWANSEA, FOR THE THIRD NIGHT IN SUCCESSION, WAS THE MAIN TARGET FOR NAZI RAIDERS, WHO RAINED HIGH-EXPLOSIVE AND FIRE BOMBS ON THE TOWN CAUSING SEVERE DAMAGE AND A NUMBER OF CASUALTIES, SOME FATAL.

As on the two previous nights, a stream of raiders dropped fire bombs indiscriminately, and then, while members of the civil defence services were working at dealing with the incendiaries, high explosives rained down.

Later came more showers of fire bombs and others again performed heroically in helping to render them harmless.

West and North-west Germany Raided

R.A.F. bombers last night attacked targets in West and North-west Germany, and invasion ports and aerodromes in enemy-occupied territory.

The raids are described by the Germans as "nuisance raids." They took place over the coastal area and Heligoland Bight.

It is said that incendiary bombs caused damage to a farm, but other bombs fell harmlessly into open country or into the sea.

It is claimed that one Wellington bomber was brought down by German naval artillery.

Damage done to a South Wales town by Nazi raiders.

BRITISH TROOPS HELD READY TO MOVE INTO GREECE
—Turkish Report

(Associated Press Message)

BELGRADE, Saturday.

With Nazi pontoons reported here to have been placed across the ice-freed Danube in preparation for a mass German military march into Bulgaria, the Turkish official radio broadcast that the British were holding large forces in North Africa in readiness for a swift sally into the Balkans via Greece.

The broadcast said that Britain was either considering the establishment of a general Balkan front or intended to prevent Greece being forced into an untimely armistice by the German thrust through Bulgaria.

Meanwhile, here in Belgrade, one diplomatic source said that the movement of Nazi troops in Bulgaria was "a matter of days, if not hours."

This source said that his staff had definitely confirmed, from first-hand observation, that a "considerable number" of Nazi bridges were already

NEW JAP MOVES REPORTED

DEFIED DEATH ON 140-MILE ABYSSINIA TREK

Aussies "Ready for Any Emergency"

The question on everyone's lips was the same: why did the Germans decide to give Swansea such a hammering?

11

Why target Swansea?

Potential target: Cwmfelin Tinplate Works.

Potential target: the shopping centre and market.

Potential target: Swansea Guildhall seen in the late 1930s.

Exactly why the Germans launched such a heavyweight attack on Swansea has never become completely clear.
It was the question on the lips of most residents 75 years ago and one that continues to be regularly asked today.

Despite the passage of time the definitive answer remains as elusive as ever. Some theories are perhaps more plausible than others. At the head of these is the fact that Swansea was a very busy seaport, vital to the war effort and the supply of food and other supplies from America and Canada in particular. It was bound to be targeted for a major raid at some point simply because of this.

Aerial reconnaissance maps and documents of the town show that the Germans, with all their thoroughness, knew exactly where all vital installations were located. It was suggested in later years that the town's docks and industries were the intended target, but that bombing aids which the Germans possessed were not accurate enough to allow them to hit such targets. In 1941, no air force had the capability of night bombing with pinpoint accuracy. So it seems Swansea as a whole was designated as the target, and if industries or docks were hit, that was a bonus for the attackers; if residential and commercial centres were hit then civilian morale would be the main casualty. In either case a significant objective would have been achieved.

German records also go some way to corroborating this theory. Nowhere in the Luftwaffe bombing reports for the Three Nights' Blitz were docks and industries specified. The target every night was simply Swansea.

Some may find that acceptable, but others raise the issue as to why the same part of the town centre was hit with a significant amount of bombs night after night, time after time.
A repeated act that appears deliberate rather than random.

Other theories suggest the target was Swansea's grain store or an ammunition train. Some speculate that the flares dropped early on in the first raid drifted off course from the docks over the town.
Others have drawn attention to the fact that the jet propulsion laboratory had been relocated to Swansea from the east coast of England. And that it was somewhere in the centre of the devastated 41 acres.

Some have fronted the theory that if the Germans had wanted to wipe Swansea out completely all they had to do was come back again . . . and again, until they did. But they didn't.

Whatever the reasons for the attack, the results were all too apparent: the Three Nights' Blitz violently erased the face of the pre-war town centre leaving the modern city centre as a direct legacy of this sad episode in Swansea's history.

The town was bloodied, but unbowed and lived on to continue its fight for survival. It was a number of years before new streets and roads began to appear, but slowly and surely the town began to raise its proud head again.

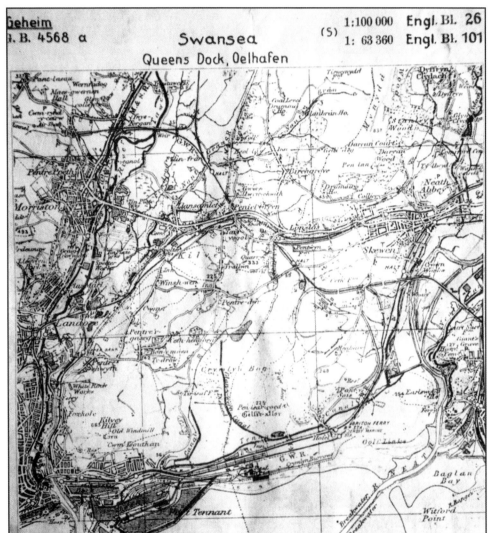

Luftwaffe maps like these helped pinpoint targets in Swansea.

98

Potential target: The huge grain warehouses of Weaver & Company dominated the eastern approach to Swansea. Today Sainsbury's and the Parc Tawe shopping and entertainment complex occupies most of this mid-1930s panorama.

A group of women munitions workers at the Landore works of Richard Thomas and Baldwin, take a break from their labours in 1940. This works too, like those near it could have been a target.

Swansea Docks shortly before the outbreak of war.

A major effort was needed
in the days immediately following
the three nights of destruction to ensure
that people were fed and watered.

12

Symbol of survival

Business as usual reads the sign on the damaged wall of this premises.

This 1960 view of Oxford Street shows the temporary Nissen-type shops built to replace the blitzed buildings.

Temporary Nissen-type shops built in Oxford Street. They remained for many years before being replaced.

Situation serious. Two words that most succinctly describe Swansea's plight after the bullying bombers had finally departed, the flames died away and the choking smoke had cleared from its streets.

After all, 41 acres of the town's commercial heart had vanished under the weight of German bombs. Essential services of electricity, gas, water and sewers, taken for granted by so many for so long were wiped out. Victims had to be sought and rescued from the damaged buildings.

A total of 171 food shops were destroyed, 64 grocers, 61 butchers, 12 bakers and 34 hotels, restaurants and cafes.

All this meant that a major effort was needed in the days immediately following the raids to ensure that people were fed. Tankers brought in water. Lorries ferried in vital supplies of bread and other essential commodities, while rest centres served up more than 25,000 meals to the hungry. There were no major supermarkets then. Small shops reigned supreme and served their customers with pride. Many of the buildings destroyed had housed provisions shops which meant that many thousands of people had nowhere to obtain essential supplies.

The market, a regular source of food for many of the townspeople had been totally destroyed. All that remained was a tangled and twisted mass of metal. In its way it could perhaps be considered Swansea's first supermarket because it was a place where, within reason, shoppers could buy almost anything they wanted. It was the hub of the town. Replacing it was top priority. In the ensuing quest to return to normality it was a problem that needed and enjoyed a speedy solution.

Within just a week, a temporary market was established on the two upper floors of the former Singleton Street bus garage, later the Grand Theatre Arts Wing. If nothing else the stalls that began trading there were an indication that life was returning to normal. A symbol of survival. And for the still troubled people, not knowing whether any further attacks were imminent this was something on which they could rebuild their routine.

Apart from this, homeless people had to be billeted with the more fortunate and the injured cared for. Then, and only then, could the huge task of clearing up and planning for the future begin.

Initially, much of the early work was devoted to clearing streets and pavements of rubble. It was a long and often difficult task. The ruins of buildings that remained in some streets were demolished by Army engineers using dynamite until all that was left was an enormous flattened area where the town had originally stood.

It might only have taken three nights to reduce to rubble a town built on the bedrock of history. It was however going to take many years before this particular phoenix would rise from its ashes.

Gower Street and Heathfield Street after the rubble had been cleared.
The area was popular with street traders who set up stalls here.

The temporary market that served Swansea until the building of the one that exists today.

THE OLD TOWN

1. St Mary's Church
2. Ben Evans department store
3. Lloyds Bank
4. Wesley Chapel
5. Market
6. Town gasworks
7. Swansea Castle
8. Mount Pleasant Church
9. Woolworth's store
10. North Dock

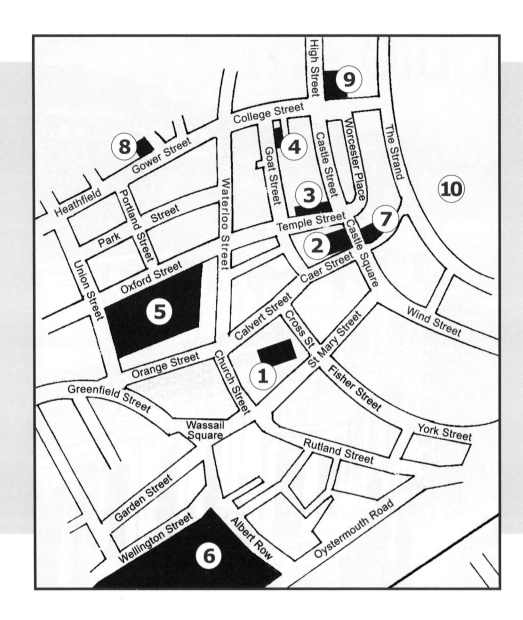

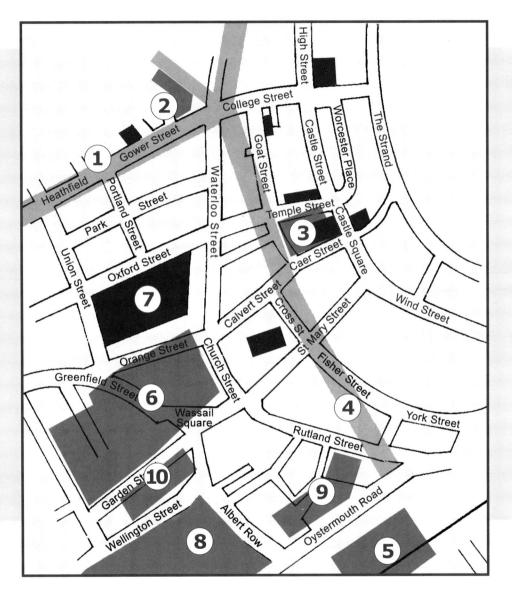

THE NEW CITY

1. The Kingsway
2. The Dragon Hotel
3. Castle Square
4. Princess Way
5. Leisure centre
6. Quadrant shopping centre
7. Market
8. Tesco supermarket
9. St David's car park
10. Garden Street car park

The terrible raids towards the end
of February 1941 were not the
first to cause distress and suffering,
nor were they to be the last.

13

Visits of destruction

A German aerial reconnaissance photograph taken after a raid on Llandarcy oil refinery.

A bomb went through the roof of this home in Sketty.

The outpatients department at Swansea hospital after a direct hit.

The terrible raids towards the end of February 1941 were not the first to cause distress and suffering to the people of Swansea town. Nor were they to be the last.
There were many more, but none were as heavy as the Three Nights' Blitz.

During the nine-month period of what has often been described as the Phoney War — from September 1939 to June 1940 — Swansea, like other British towns, had been left in almost complete peace. However, when France fell in the summer of 1940, airfields in Brittany and along the French side of the English Channel became available to the Germans.

Swansea was well within the range of these newly won airfields and perhaps because of the high ranking the Germans gave to its port it is no surprise the first attacks on the town began soon after, in June 1940. Throughout the Second World War,

Swansea was subject to air raids on 44 separate occasions, the majority of these were minor, but, there were six more serious raids.

There were two main phases of bombings: June to October, 1940 and January to November, 1941, while 1942 and 1943 each witnessed only one attack.

In the summer and autumn of 1940, Swansea was victim to a number of hit-and-run forays by individual or small numbers of aircraft. Some of the raids were in daylight, but few did serious damage. However, on September 1, 1940 the town had its first major experience of war. This visit by the Luftwaffe was a foretaste of what was to come. In a prolonged raid there was extensive damage, 33 people were killed and 105 injured.

German defeat in the Battle of Britain brought some respite, but in January, 1941 the raids began again. This time Swansea was targeted as a Battle of the Atlantic port. Some light raids early in the month were followed by a more serious blitz on January 17.

This was the town's heaviest raid to that point. In all 58 tons of high explosives and some incendiaries resulted in 58 deaths and 97 people suffering injury. After this Swansea was left alone for just over a month until the Luftwaffe launched its infamous Three Nights' Blitz.

During the bombing campaigns many of the town's suburbs were the subject of sporadic attacks.

The Eastside suffered on a number of occasions, probably because of its close proximity to the docks. Activities there were hit and disruption caused frequently. On one occasion in a daylight raid a lone aircraft caused serious damage at the docks.

Bombs were also dropped on Morriston, Hafod, Mayhill, Treboeth, Cwmbwrla, Manselton, Brynhyfryd and Dunvant. Houses around Sketty and Ffynone received direct hits but many bombs fell into the sea from West Cross around Mumbles Head to the bays of Langland and Caswell.

That was bad luck for the bombers, but certainly not for Swansea.

One of the houses at Teilo Crescent,
Mayhill, that suffered a direct hit.

This wrecked dockside loading crane was the result of another visit by the Luftwaffe bombers.

Calendar of the

1940

JUNE

27 First raid 3.3Oam. Danygraig hit by six high explosive (HE) bombs.

29 Early morning. Lone raider dropped two HE bombs in Morriston.

JULY

10 King's Dock hit. Extensive damage, 12 dockers killed, 26 injured.

18 Nine HE dropped on railway sidings at Jersey Marine.

20 Unexploded bomb (UXB) reported in Danygraig. HE in South Dock.

22 Two HE dropped on farm at Cockett.

27 Two HE dropped on breakwater at Swansea docks.

30 Two HE on Cockett.

AUGUST

2 11pm 14 HE and incendiary bombs (IB) dropped across town. Four injured.

3 Two HE and IBs dropped on Waunarlwydd, some in sea off West Cross.

6 10 HE dropped in sea off West Cross.

10/11 31 HE in one-hour raid. Railway viaduct at Landore hit. Houses damaged in Manselton, Cwmbwrla and Brynhyfryd — 13 killed, 15 injured.

16 HE dropped in sea off Mumbles Head.

17 16 HE dropped in Hafod, Cwmbwrla, Treboeth and Cadle. One injured.

18 12 HE fell near Cwmbwrla School, Llangyfelach Street. One killed, two injured.

24 Incendiary bombs scattered from Kilvey Hill to Dunvant.

SEPTEMBER

1/2 251 HE, 1,000 IB dropped, scattered over large areas of town. Extensive damage

—33 killed, 36 badly injured, 69 hurt.

3 Two HE dropped in Crymlyn Brook.

4/5 Four HE dropped on farmland at Llansamlet.

11 Lone raider dropped three HE on Langland Terrace, Brynmill.

24 Two HE dropped, one in River Tawe north of St Thomas at New Cut Bridge, one in centre of King's Dock. IB dropped across Rutland Street and Wind Street.

25 Nine HE and incendiaries fell on Uplands, Mayhill.

bombing raids

OCTOBER

9 Six HE and IB fell across docks, Eastside and Morriston.

21 15 HE and IB dropped on Townhill, Winchwen, Cockett, Mayhill and Llansamlet.

Five injured.

1941

JANUARY

2 Two HE fell in field at Ynystawe.

4/5 12 HE and 200 IB across town —20 injured.

13 One HE in King's Dock Road. Three injured.

17 100 HE and up to 7,000 IB dropped—55 dead, 38 seriously injured, 59 hurt.

FEBRUARY

19/20/21 Three Nights' Blitz — 230 dead, more than 400 injured.

MARCH

3 Four HE dropped on Cefn Coed. One injured.

4 12 HE dropped on foreshore between Mumbles and Swansea.

12 13 HE dropped on Crymlyn Bog and Hafod — three killed, nine hurt.

14 100 IB scattered over Bonymaen and Llansamlet.

24 Two HE dropped on Danygraig and two HE in Crymlyn Bog.

31 One HE dropped on Strand Power House. One HE in North Dock. Three killed.

APRIL

8 800 IB dropped at Limeslade and Mumbles Head. One HE at Plunch Lane.

22 Two parachute mines at Frederick Place, Llansamlet — 13 injured.

MAY

20 One HE direct hit on Neath Road School, Morriston, injuring three.

31 Four HE fell between Pengwern Road and Morriston Park injuring four.

JUNE

28 Two NE fell in sea between Langland and Caswell. UXB in Mayhill Gardens.

NOVEMBER

28 Two parachute mines. One fell at the junction of The Strand and Welcome Lane; the other near the Burrows Inn, Port Tennant. One killed, 23 injured.

1942

JULY

2 Around 240 IB fell on Birchgrove area. No damage or casualties.

1943

FEBRUARY

16 Nine planes attack for half an hour—34 killed, 111 wounded, 61 severely. 800 houses damaged.

MAY

15 Last air raid alert.

It took just three nights of bombing
to destroy the old Swansea
and three decades for a new town
to rise up in its place.

14

Rising from the ashes

The Kingsway one of the main new roads created as Swansea rose again.

Work underway on the rebuilding of St Mary's Parish Church.

A web of timbers forms the roof of new buildings of Caer Street.

Today, like most 21st Century cities Swansea is continually evolving. This is to keep pace with modern day demands for new shops, offices and homes. Such a gradual metamorphosis is however, much different to the redevelopment which followed the Three Nights' Blitz.

Today there is always something for planners and architects to work with, blend into or rise above, but all that remained then was a vast, wide open space. In a way it was a blank canvas for those tasked with redevelopment.

The months following the concentrated bombing of 1941 saw extensive logistical problems such as re-housing the homeless and clearing dangerous sites. The first opportunity for redeveloping the town centre did not come until 1944 and the initial work of clearing the bombed sites began soon afterwards. It would however be decades before these scars were completely healed. The big question was how should the town be put back together? This created something of dilemma for the council.

There was a fundamental issue to be decided and that was whether Swansea should be rebuilt on the old homely, familiar lines or should a new conception of a better, bigger town be adopted. Eventually it was agreed to plan boldly and create a modem metropolis. The decision meant that many of the old streets and buildings vanished forever — and, with them, much of Swansea's character.

Some emergency reconstruction took place while the war was still going on. A makeshift open air market was constructed, and 20 Nissen hut shops were erected. Real reconstruction finally started in the early 1950s.

The rebirth was a long, painful affair, complicated by post war shortages, building regulations and red tape. In 1946, compulsory purchase orders were made to acquire the blitzed sites and rebuilding got underway with the promise of a shopping precinct.

In November 1950, Princess Margaret opened The Kingsway. Two years later, Princess Way opened. As the new Swansea took shape, it attracted the attention of chain stores and the first major shop to open — in 1952 — was C&A in Portland Street. The former David Evans store reopened in 1954 in Princess Way, near its old site, but Ben Evans, remained fairly grand at a Walter Road location for some years and its old site became what is now Castle Square.

Nothing was plain sailing as the new town slowly took shape. Completion of the covered market was delayed until 1961 and as for the promised shopping precinct it was 30 years before the Quadrant finally opened to shoppers in 1979.

Since then many other significant changes have taken place. Shopping has moved out of town in many cases. The Marina and SA1 developments with their offices and housing have overtaken much of the docklands and along the way, in 1969, the sleepy old town became a proud new city.

This steel skeleton, towering over the Kingsway roundabout, was to become the Dragon Hotel.

This became the Kingsway, but until the blitz it was known as Heathfield Street. Craddock Street is on the left and Union Street on the right. This picture was taken in 1948. The regeneration had begun.

Looking over the rooftops as St Mary's Church is reborn. The building is framed in scaffolding.

Now occupied by McDonalds this building, one of the first to be completed after the war originally housed Boots the chemist. Castle Gardens, latterly replaced by Castle Square is in front.

Looking along St Helen's Road in 1948, from its junction with Page Street, towards what became the Kingsway.

By the late 1950s Swansea's future could be seen sprouting everywhere. Here, the adventurous new framework of Swansea market is pieced together as the decade drew to a close.

The finger-like structures of part of Swansea's rapidly changing 21st Century skyline. A far cry from the type of buildings that existed in the dark days of the Second World War. Alongside is a modern day marina panorama.